Methods of Western State Secret Services in 1998-2008: Use of Stooges (Patsies), Stalking with Cars, Sleep Deprivation, Toxins, and Pain

Artour Rakhimov

Table of Contents

Introduction

This book contains my older writings (1998-2008) about the activities of Western security intelligence organizations (secret agents representing "national security") and what happened in my life during these years. In particular, I describe activities of secret agents from CSIS (Canadian Security Intelligence Service), FBI (Federal Bureau of Investigation from the USA), Garda (Secret Police in Ireland), MI6 (Military Intelligence 6 or British national security organization), Algemene Inlichtingen-en Veiligheidsdienst (AIVD) (Secret Service of the Netherlands), and Veilighad van de Staat (national security of Belgium). For comparison, the book also includes my 1991-1992 personal real-life experiences with KGB agents.

The book described the following typical techniques to influence the mind of the target (me):

1) use of patsies (or stooges) on police cars, fire trucks, ambulances with sirens, garbage removal trucks, and mass display using hundreds of cars of ordinary people

2) noise harassment when the target is at home (not on city streets or outside)

3) use of snaps in private rooms of the target to create extreme sleep deprivation

4) use of gases to create various required effects on the mind and behavior of the target

5) use of poisons to destroy health of the target.

These old writings have grammatical mistakes. I am sorry about this.

All chapters of this book were written before 2009, while this introduction was written many years later, in 2023. The largest article of this book (Chapter 1), together with other articles and documents present in this book, was also sent by me in numerous letters to various officials who deal with human rights located in Canada, the USA, and various European countries.

Because of the activities of Canadian secret agents during those years, especially snap-type noises (including noises at night) in rooms where I stayed, as well as other harassment techniques, in the following years, starting from 1998, I, as a Canadian citizen, 13 times applied for political asylum in 7 Western countries.

Also, years later, in December of 2019, I finally discovered the root of my numerous serious physical, emotional, and cognitive problems that suddenly started, as out of nowhere, in 1998. The hair analysis test for heavy metals done by a German lab showed that my mercury level was 10 times above the upper limit. That explained why in 1998 I suddenly developed numerous health problems which later resulted in kidney failure, liver failure, serious GI problems (IBD, gastroparesis, etc.), and declining health for over 20 years. This condition is also known as "mad hatter syndrome".

In 2.5 years of more targeted treatment, in June 2022, the mercury level in my hair dropped 50 times, to 5 times below the upper limit, and now I am dealing with over 20 years of mercury poisoning.

As for the mental or cognitive effects of mercury, I can certainly claim that I remember my personal life events from the

1980s until 1998 much better than events that took place with me from 1999 until about 2021.

Since 2009 and during the following years, there were many changes in national security organizations, while certain principles of their function remain unchanged.

One of my greatest discoveries of the last decade was that when some secret agents use poisons and/or destroy the health of the target and/or are involved in real-life activities that are criminal in the normal world, other secret agents are obliged to remain silent about wrongdoings of their colleagues in their special security intelligence world.

Again, my sincere apologies for grammatical mistakes in these old documents written by me over 15 years ago.

Chapter 1. Personal experience about war on terrorism, as it is practiced by national security agencies

Keywords: national security, secret agency, intelligence service, secret police, state security, terrorism, war on terrorism, secrecy, hiding villain effect, fear, threat, suspect, secret agent, paranoia, harassment, special methods, persecution, stalking, torture, intimidation, pain, dehumanization, depersonalization, violence, human rights, justice, non-violent resistance, cooperation, peace.

NSAs (national security agencies) are created to deal with threats to national security and fight terrorism and large criminal activities. According to laws and practice of world largest countries, like the USA, the UK, Canada, and others, NSAs use special methods in order to achieve these goals. If one visits an office of any NSA, it would be impossible to get answers about details of the special methods used by the secret agents.

Since I have been one of those threats for over 10 years, I decided to present here my experience about these special methods used by CSIS (Canadian Security Intelligence Service) in Canada, and their colleagues, state security agents of the USA, the UK, Holland, Belgium, Ireland, and Italy. I visited those countries avoiding poisoning and harassment. Sometimes, when independent living was too difficult, I applied for political asylum there, as a Canadian citizen, about 10 times, but instead of help got a special treatment described below.

1.1 Night noises method

Real events, Toronto, 1996-1997. Sleep deprivation can be arranged using pulsing noise generated every 3-5 minutes. Imagine that it is late and the person wants to sleep. He goes to bed. After he closes his eyes, he hears loud clicking noise (a crispy sound similar to cracking in fires or breaking wood pieces) originated from the table in his room. While the single click may be (?) an accidental event, 3-5 minutes later, when the person almost falls asleep, there is another click. Due to desire to sleep, the person wants to resolve the problem. He approaches the table in order to find out the source of environmental pollution. The next crispy sound comes from the opposite corner of the room. The man goes there. Then the sound comes from the ceiling. Later the chair near the table produces noise. Since the person wants to sleep and the problem is still unsolved, he uses ear plugs, but the noise gets louder. After some hours of useless attempts and in the state of exasperation and fatigue, the person manages to fall asleep for remaining few hours. In the morning he has to go to his job. His job is teaching math in a private high school in Toronto.

During the next night the story is repeated. The man tries to go to the kitchen, but the noise chases him there. Other tenants of the house also get curious since they hear the noise through their closed doors. After several sleepless nights, as sleep deprivation experiments found, people start to hallucinate. As it should be, he, indeed, sees small fires in various places. His concentration, memory and many other skills deteriorate, so that simple jobs are hard to do. Teaching in a high school obviously needs some interpersonal and other skills. The person invites police to visit his house at about 2-3 am. During presence of 2 police officers for about 1 hour, the house and the room are absolutely quiet. When the police officers leave, the noises re-appear.

Later the person, due to noises, moves out and rents another room. Before moving-in, he inquired the new landlord and other tenants about presence of any noises. All testified that the house has been quiet for over 20 years. The person checked the room for about 1 hour while reading a book. The room was quiet. The man moves into the new place. In about 5-7 days, the noises and the story start over again. During last 10 years, the person, mainly due to noises, changed his place of housing about 10 times. While words can describe only some part of the whole picture, one can try to experience such events just for few days in order to have better understanding of the effects.

Sources of the noise. Obviously, the noises were man-made while the reactions of the person were observed in hidden cameras so that the noise sources could not be discovered. Later, the man visits a Professor of Physics at the University of Toronto with background in electromagnetic waves. The professor explains that such noises can be generated by special tiny devices inserted into holes or cracks of any object (like a chair, table, etc.). The device reacts to high-frequency electromagnetic impulse send from outside. Its principle of work is similar to cell phones. The generated noises can be very crisp and loud, as if large tree branches are broken or a small gun is fired.

Secret noise harassment. A similar special method is based on the pulsed noise generated only during sleep. As British studies on volunteers revealed, it is possible to generate noises that do not wake up the person, but prevent him from having deep stages of sleep. Normally, the person has transition from a shallow to a deeper sleep stage (stage 2) after 10-15 minutes. Normally, in about 60-80 minutes the person reaches the deepest sleep stages, and the cycle starts all over again from REM (rapid eye movements) stage. Application of pulsing noise every 10-15 minutes results in shifts to more shallow sleep for the whole night. The person cannot reach deep sleep stages. Deep stages, on the other hand, are characterized by thorough relaxation of skeletal muscles and appearance of special slow waves in the brain. Absence of deep sleep stages means absence of proper rest for the brain and the muscles. After awakening, the person cannot recall hearing any noises, but the quality of sleep was miserable and he feels like after nightmares. What are the consequences?

Effects of night noise harassment. Daily behavior is characterized by sleepiness, more irritable mood, worsened memory, poor coordination and other physiological, mental and psychological disturbances. If the method is applied for several nights in row, the person can be on the verge of the psychological breakdown due to neurosis. The person gets particularly stressed by the similar or other noises even when they are natural and produced by usual devices and appliances.

The method can be applied during a part of the night, but for weeks or months. In this case, depending on various factors, the person gets partially physically, mentally and psychologically incapacitated. Generally, this method alone can reduce the person to the vegetable state. The person experienced these effects of night harassment in Canada, the Netherlands, and Belgium.

Experimental studies on animals showed that if noises are present during every night, the animals lose their appetite and weight, and gradually die from psychological and physiological exhaustion. Hence, we are talking here about the lethal weapon that is routinely used by secret agents, but which is officially not denounced or forbidden. Probably, there are no treaties or agreements, as well as national laws, against this technique.

1.2 Daily noise harassment

The person can be also persistently attacked during day times by noises from various devices and appliances in his house, his computer, sirens from ambulance, fire department and police special vehicles, noises from motorcycles, and other devices and sources used by the proxies.

Real events. Toronto, Ontario. 2000-2001. A high school teacher, after night harassment described above, wants to find a quiet place to have a short nap during a school break. He goes in an empty classroom, and closes his eyes; at that moment he hears clicking noise. (Since the NSAs hire only people with superior intelligence, the agents anticipated that the person may try to rest in certain places, and installed noise devices in such places). The person goes to a quiet street, which, as all of the sudden, is filled by roaring Harley motorcycles due to arrival of a group of proxies (in this case Hells Angels bikers). Few days later, he is in the forest. Silence, after weeks of noises, sounds like a paradise. Well, in several minutes, other proxies on a helicopter start hovering just above him.

The person hears sirens every 10-20 minutes while traveling to and from his job, shopping, traveling during weekends, etc. He walks along a usually quiet street. In several places, as if all of the sudden, local gardeners-proxies start their mowing devices and chain saws. The proxies start noises when he is closest to them. Clicking noises also accompany his street walk. The clicks are "accidentally" from cars, lamp posts, phone booths, and other sources, since his regular routes of walking and traveling are known to the agents.

He reads a book in his room. When he turns to the next page, he hears a crispy click. Turning to the next page about 1-2 minutes later is also accompanied by noise. Later, it happens few more times. Such noises also need to be experienced in practice in order to appreciate their effects.

When he goes to a library in order to read a book and other papers, the noise "follows" him there too (because the agents knew where he could go). Moreover, library reading is accompanied by "cleaning harassment". That means that when he starts reading, cleaning staff proxies start mopping floor, removing dust and perform other seemingly regular operations around the reading person. The key is that these operations should start not in according with regular cleaning schedule, but only when the person arrives there. The "cleaning harassment" is more effective, when it is done on constant bases so that in many places the cleaning staff of different places (near his house, work, shopping, walking, etc.) get involved in their job activities, as a part of the special methods, in front of the person.

Real events. St. Martin Latem, Gent region, Belgium; May-June 2005. Noises follow the person in his room, kitchen shared with other asylum seekers, and washroom. In order to avoid noises, the person goes to a neighboring park. In about 20 minutes the park is filled with proxies and machinery for mowing and doing other landscaping jobs. He goes to another small park. After about 15 quiet minutes, mowing and other activities are started by proxies near the house adjacent to this park. Later, the person goes to another remote place in order to read the book and have rest. The place in a few minutes is visited by proxies on motorcycles that have their mufflers removed. This special security technique allows even small motorcycles to produce roaring noises. Each 5-10 minutes the place is visited by new proxies on motorcycles with no mufflers.

This description generates many questions, e.g.: Who could organize that and how? The only sensible explanation is following. Practical organization of these events was based on personal meetings of the secret agents with involved people. Claiming importance of national security and using the label of the state agency, the secret agents got support of various proxies, including authorities of city cleaning, garbage collecting, ambulance, police, and fire prevention services. All these proxies must be informed about exclusive importance of these special operations and their superior secrecy. Probably the proxies sign a special secret Oath of Secrecy. It provides the agency with protection from enquiries, commissions, visits of human right activists, lawsuits, and other nuisances and problems. Indeed, somebody may decide to challenge the legacy of these special methods. In this case, the involved proxies could claim that they just did their regular jobs.

Effects of daily noise harassment. Persistent attacks with noises, with involvement of other state services and private individuals change the concerns and thoughts of the person. Instead of analyzing and solving his real life problems involving, for example, employment, relatives, friends, housing, and hobbies, the person gets preoccupied with this demonstration of force and its effects on him and his health. When the degree of harassment is very high, the person can get various health problems, depending on his genetic predisposition, diet, and other factors. Daily noise harassment is more effective when it is combined with night noises and can lead to psychological stress, psychosis, depression, and neurosis.

General harassment campaign by proxies and the agents

Toronto. 1997. The person, because of night noises, theft of employment, and other acts of the CSIS, decides to seek help and protect his rights. He visits, using his bike, the CHRC (Canadian Human Right Commission) that has an office in Toronto Downtown area. During the visit, he asks help of the CHRC and asks them to answer simple questions related to human rights. When he leaves the CHRC building, he encounters fire department cars with sirens The trip back home is not long (about 20 minutes), but traveling further he sees and hears ambulance cars with sirens. During the whole night, police cars circle around the block where he lives. The room is full of loud clicking noises so that he cannot get normal sleep even when using industrial ear-protectors together with ear-plugs to reduce the effect of noises. Early in the morning, when he goes to his work, he finds out that there is a dead squirrel lying in front of the house where he rents the room. Both tires of his bike are flat.

Dublin. Ireland. 1998. The person applies for political asylum in Ireland and lives in the hostel for asylum seekers. Meals were prepared in the kitchen and were eaten there. The person cooked his meal and started to eat. Another asylum seeker comes to him and asks 2 cents, shortage of cash for the telephone call... Some minutes later, another asylum seeker comes and ask 1 cent for a telephone call. Later, one more. During the next meal, the person decides to eat outside in the park nearby. He goes there and starts to eat. Few minutes later, a stranger comes and asks the time. Few minutes later there is another one in need of time. Later again. The situation, with some variations (e.g., places and faces), keeps repeating day after day for each meal many days in row.

Amsterdam, the Netherlands; June 2004. The person arrives to Amsterdam in the morning. Near the railway station he is met with 3 large garbage trucks that appear just in front of the person so that he has to go between them in order to reach a hostel where he wants to stay. On the way to the hostel, during about 10 min walk, another garbage truck was backing up in such a way that to be just in front of the person. When the man finally reaches the hostel, located on a narrow street, another garbage truck was blocking almost the whole street, so that the person has to squeeze between the street and the truck. Since the hostel reservation "accidentally" is unavailable, the person was send to another hostel. On the way, the story with proxies on garbage trucks is repeated. Apart from garbage trucks, several proxies on motorcycles accelerate without mufflers, so that they produce roaring noise when passing the person.

Real events. Gent, Belgium; June 2005. While spending about 3-4 hours in the central part of Gent (a large city in Belgium), the person "accidentally" encounters several groups of proxies on motorcycles, over 10 garbage trucks, several cars with their sirens, and city cleaning cars.

"Many ordinary cars trick"

In some situations, for example, during weekends or in quiet areas of the city, it is more difficult for the agents to sue garbage trucks, noisy motorcycles, ambulances or fire department cars with sirens. How to harass or intimidate the person? The geniuses from national securities invented the following technique which is nicely combined with migraine headaches and sleep deprivation.

Cork 2007. The person rides a bike using small streets with only local access traffic during a very quiet Sunday morning (about 8-9 am). When the person passes near one car, this car's engine is started by the owner. 50 m later, there is another car that is started just when the person passes nearby. Then 70 m later again... Later again.... During 20-30 minutes ride on the bike the agents employed about 40-50 people each of whom performed a small and seemingly "innocent" thing: they started their cars when the agents send them a phone message to do so. Timing is important for this operation.

In many Canadian, American, Dutch, and Irish cities many hundreds car owners were involved in such operations during one day. On a psychological level, such tremendous mass activity indicates strong public disapproval, while the agent watching in the camera feels like a super-king: he is moving a huge army of proxies all of whom "express" and carry their spirit of war on terrorism when they are involved in such operations. (By the way the chances of car accidents, with these proxies, are probably about 10-30 times higher than in ordinary situations.)

In other situations, the agents can flood streets or parks where the "controlled" person arrives with dog owners. Try to imagine: dozens of dog owners, due to instructions if secret agents flood the route of travel of the "controlled" subject. Obviously, the agents feel themselves safe when there are hundreds or thousands people obey the agents and harass and disapprove the "controlled" subject. Moreover, such public disapproval creates good psychological foundation for drugging: if so many people disapprove the person, it would make sense to "execute" the will of masses by drugging or poisoning or radiating the person. Hence, these mass activities also represent self-assertion and self-deification of the secret agents.

Obviously, presence of these activities is easy to check since thousands of people do a "small innocent" thing: obey wild fantasies of the secret agents. Clearly, the agents never tell to these proxies that there are hundreds or thousands of them are used for this activity. Moreover, each proxy is likely to create a fantasy that he/she has some ultra important and special mission, especially taking into account that proxies do not see each other and have no idea about the mass scale of the harassment.

1.3 Vandalism

NSA agents study habits, typical routes and whereabouts of the person. The person notices that a big window of the next house is smashed. (It will not be repaired for many days due to requests of the agents). A car that appeared on the opposite side of the street is severely damaged. (This car is to be there for weeks). Renovations by proxies (with machinery for road repair and destruction of existing structures) become a typical tool of the agents. The effect of vandalism is to interfere with existing order, harmony, naturalness, and peacefulness of existing places and events so that the person experience confusion, fear, stress, and anxiety.

Psychological and neurological effects of general harassment campaigns and vandalism can be various depending on the variety of factors. If the person has any health problems, such campaign can trigger his gastrointestinal, cardiovascular and many other problems and concerns. If he was healthy before, could he "accidentally" get these health problems?

Cork. Ireland. 2006. The person is to move and live in a new room. The house is filled with various devices and appliances that are broken or malfunctioning. The lamps in corridors, toilets, and his room are not working. The existing shower, toilet sink, drying machine, handles of windows are tampered with in the way to make their normal use difficult or impossible.

1.4 Drugging

While use of toxic and poisonous chemicals by military, police and other state services and agencies is forbidden (or strictly regulated) by international and domestic laws, including responsibility for any damage to other people, the NSAs do not have laws that restrict the use of poisonous, toxic and other damage-producing chemicals.

Real events. Toronto. 1997. The person has had an excellent health in the past. He has been actively engaged in endurance sports (like running and cross country skiing) including daily training and participation in national and international competitions. His sport results were sufficient for him to qualify for a Canadian national team. Then the person, on a daily basis, unknowingly gets methyl mercury with his food. The initial symptoms include diarrhea, metallic taste in the mouth, and headaches. Since the agents observed the person in hidden cameras, they choose such a dose so that he can still work and be physically active, but the quality of these activities becomes poor. When the person visits his relatives and eats with them, he feels OK and abnormal symptoms disappear. After about 2-3 years of drugging, the person cannot exercise and compete. He has frequent colds and infections (every 1-2 weeks); his blood sugar gets poorly regulated. He experiences urinary incontinence, chronic diarrhea, daily headaches, problems with sleep, unstable mood and other concerns.

Creation of gastrointestinal problems is currently among popular methods of NSAs. During medieval times some people invented the following method of punishment (or torture). The person was fed with a meal, one end of a long rope with knots. After 1-2 hours the rope was vigorously pulled out. As the result of this action, the person may die or would not be able to eat until the guts restore their structural integrity. Healing may be impossible. Modern toxicology made the use of this method much easier for the agents.

Real events. Toronto. 1997-2003. The person is secretly fed, with his food, chemicals that cause intestinal damage, inflammation and acute immune response. Persistent use of these toxins results in appearance of ulcers, chronic diarrhea, burping, gases, pain and other effects. When the person buys and eats food (without leaving it at home or overnight), he has no problems. Food that was left, even for a while, causes problems. He visits relatives and sometimes eats with others – no problems again.

Real events. New Castle. Great Britain. 2001. The person is secretly given a combination of toxic bacteria and chemicals that causes acute severe GI distress so that the person gets oral thrush, severe diarrhea, burping, gas, and pain under the stomach. The degree of damage to digestive organs is so strong that he cannot normally run or walk since shaking of the gastrointestinal organs causes diarrhea, burping, pain, and gases. Just one jump or sudden jerk of the body leads to flare-up with diarrhea and other symptoms. Riding a bike or traveling in a vehicle (e.g., a bus, tram, or car) is a big problem. Usual brushing of teeth is not anymore possible since shaking causing flare up. The person cannot eat greens, skin of fruits or vegetables, raw fruits, and nuts. In fact, only soft and cooked foods are well tolerated. With time, the person develops gluten intolerance and eating bread leads to worsening of digestive problems. Diagnosis of the problem could take more than 1 year in the UK due to long list of people waiting for endoscopies and other methods of medical diagnosis of GI problems.

In order to make the recovery from digestive problems impossible, the agents put the eggs of intestinal worms in his food. After hatching and maturation inside his body, infestation with round worms (Ascaris family) resulted in weight loss, depression, unstable mood and other problems. After the man successfully eliminated worms, the agents again put eggs of their secret helpers in his food.

Apart from creating digestive problems, British agents use toxic gases that produce excruciating headache, dizziness, loss of coordination and concentration, irritability, diarrhea, and other neurological and physiological effects. The toxic gases also cause severe thirst since the toxin is cleared from the blood by the kidneys. That drug causes polyuria (production of large quantities of urine) and the man needs to drink, during days of drugging, from about 5 up to 20 l of water in order to eliminate severe thirst and restore water balance. Repetitive use of such poisonous chemicals results in kidney disease. The person develops diabetes insipidus (abnormal thirst) that is officially diagnosed in 2002 and chronic kidney disease.

Gas NX. Great Britain. 2002. The person discovers a following relationship. There were many days when he had severe headaches, polyuria, and strong thirst with drinking of large quantities of water. During the previous nights he always waked up in the middle of the nights (about 3 a.m., the most favorite agents' time) due to the desire to pee, but only a few drops of urine were produced. Later, he understood that gas NX starts to produce noticeable symptoms in about 12 hours. The headache was excruciating and stronger than, for example, during the neuralgia of the triple face nerve that he experienced in the past.

Real events. Toronto. 2002-2003. The person tries to get rid of his digestive problems. He consults a medical gastroenterologist, does endoscopies, and is prescribed medication. He buys food supplements, vitamins and minerals in order to create conditions for gut recovery. Normally, healing would take some weeks or months. The secret agents observe improvements (e.g., less burping, less diarrhea, and improved mood) and add toxic chemicals to his food. This nullifies his previous progress. The person starts to carry all his food with him so that it cannot be poisoned. The agents then start to use toxic gases that cause, apart from headaches, GI problems. (Many warfare gases, apart from neurological symptoms, cause diarrhea, vomiting and other effects.) The agents also use chemicals, which are, when in contact with skin, to cause diarrhea and other digestive problems even in healthy people.

Since the person is easily accessible during the night (he is sleeping, after "accidental" loss of employment, in a shelter for homeless), the CSIS agents, first, use sleeping gas, that paralyses the person, and then put eggs of worms in his mouth. That makes digestive recovery impossible. The person starts to learn parasitology and acquires skills in this area. He can, using the microscope, identify eggs of different types of worms and knows how to eliminate worms using various medical, herbal and natural substances and techniques. In response, the agents use special strain of worms that is resistant to any conventional medication.

Chronic presence of worms causes severe systemic Candidasis (overgrowth of Candida Albicanis, a fungus that feeds on simple sugars). A glass of juice or two teaspoons of table sugar causes a rise in blood glucose with appearance of skin rashes, skin itching, thirst and other symptoms of the disease (systemic Candidasis) typical for the last stage of AIDS.

Repetitive use of poisonous gases results in kidney failure. For several days in row the person normally drinks water, but since urinary output is less than 200 ml per day, the person accumulates the water in the body gaining about 4 kg of extra weight. That causes high blood pressure, headaches, fainting and emergency hospitalization. With failing kidneys, the person travels to Finland where he fasts on water for 12 days in order to restore filtering abilities of kidneys' nephrons. However, when the man comes back to Toronto, the use of gases again results in kidney's failure. Fasting in Toronto slightly improves the work of his kidneys and the output of urine, but the use of toxins again blocks the kidneys. These secret treatments are combined with psychological harassment, and night noises.

Real events. Amsterdam. 2003-2005. Dutch secret agents observe that the person makes attempts to recover from GI problems. Instead of very slow walking and eating only baby food, the person walks normally and can tolerate, for example, raw fruits and nuts. This improvement in health is undesirable for the agents and the agents put toxic chemicals in his food supplements. The GI problems appear again and get worse. In order to ensure chronic diarrhea, burping, gases, and intestinal pain, the agents systematically put chemicals in his food.

Use of neurological toxins causes another kidney failure. The chemical attack is combined with night noises campaigns and general methods of harassment. The person is mentally incapacitated due to loss of concentration and cognitive impairment caused by drugging, night noises, harassment and other special methods.

Gas BX. Real events. Belgium. May-June 2005. Due to digestive problems the person can not walk. He rides his bike in order to move around. On many occasions the person experiences thirst, headache, and digestive problems after riding the bike. Apart from the headache, when the weather is not warm, he also gets cold hands and feet. He notices that this happens only after he rides his bike in places with no people, after a certain car passes near him. If he rides only in the places where other people are present, the headache and other symptoms do not appear. Later, he checks this idea and notices that the headache appears in 30 minutes after the encounter with this special car.

1.5 More recent events

Cork (Ireland). April 2006. The person is sometimes visited by his friends and acquaintances. The clothes of these visitors are sprayed by secret agents with chemicals that produce allergic reaction in the person causing autoimmune response and intestinal inflammation. Other people do not notice or feel the effect of the chemical.

Santa Monica, San Francisco, Palo Alto (all California), Vancouver (Washington, USA). May-September 2006. The US agents use night noises (to prevent normal sleep), harassment using noisy cars, control of ventilation in buildings, helicopters, sirens of police, ambulance, fire department cars to bother, harass, damage and intimidate the person.

Toronto. October-November 2006. Now, when the person suffers from allergies and sensitivity to air quality, the agents create heavy traffic just near him. How? By controlling traffic lights, organizing congestions using proxies who drive large cars, trucks or buses, and by directing other people to drive using certain routes. Normally, small streets of Toronto may have only 1-2 cars per minute or less. However, the agents can increase the local traffic up to 10-20 cars every minute. Moreover, in order to intensify the effect, many cars send by agents have malfunctioning mufflers that produce loud noise. The agents also instruct other drivers to turn on music loudly. The popular choices of the agents are heavy rock, metal, or rap. The agents also ask some drivers to turn the lower frequencies of the music on maximum so that the body of the car starts to vibrate.

After numerous examples of stalking, the person visits the Police Station #52 in Downtown of Toronto. He is met with a group of about 4-5 police officers. He describes them the situation. They take his address, phone number, promising to send police to investigate and ... never get back to him. On Monday, October 30, 2006 he again visits the same police station. This time, the female officer (Badge #8871) send him to RCMP since as she and other officers said Toronto police do not investigate such "intelligent crimes". The person makes telephone calls to RCMP (1-800-387 0020) and reports about the crimes. The receptionists write his address and phone number and ... never get back. It looks as if Ontario Provincial Police, Royal Canadian Mountain Police and the CSIS formed a criminal alliance.

The person rents his own room. He notices that when he is in his room or in the kitchen, only 1-2 cars may pass near the house. However, when he goes outside (for a walk, ride, shopping, job, etc.), he is always met by a pack of about 7-10 cars that appear just when he leaves the house. The agents use this "meeting" effect either to create fumes (causing migraine for him) of, due to other, e.g. psychological reasons.

He visits police station #14 (Toronto West) and reports about the crimes. The police officers and their chief all refuse to investigate, while agreeing that such activities (directing cars) are illegal. They also claim that RCMP should take care about such crimes since, as they say "CSIS is a federal organization, while OPP deals with provincial problems." How and why they surely decided that the crimes were committed by the state security agents is unclear. (Probably they knew that only CSIS agents get state power and logistic to organize these crimes.)

The agents use special gas against the person, but only in special situations, e.g., when the person goes to see the doctor or make blood tests. The gas causes thirst, racing heart (up to 20-30 beats increase in heart rate), and exceptional irritability, in addition to headaches. The gas is also used when the person tries to get involved in Christianity-related activities (visiting or going to churches, Bible-study groups, etc.) and when he eats soy products. It was typical for the agents in the past to condition him against certain foods. How? The person eats something and about 30-60 min later agents creates headaches using gases, as if the food is to blame. Now, when his kidneys are bad, he does not eat animal proteins, beans are too rough for his inflames intestines and the agents target soy products.

February-March 2007. Pisa (Italy). Italian secret agents used electromagnetic radiation and allergens causing headaches, bloating, diarrhea, fatigue, and other negative symptoms. They also employed hundreds of cars and motorcycles for daytime harassment, especially when I was on streets, going shopping, etc.

May-June 2008. Santa Monica, Los Angeles, Pacific Palisades, West Los Angeles, San Jose, Palo Alto (all California, USA). FBI agents organized sleep deprivation, migraine headaches, and gastrointestinal stress. It was particularly important for them, for some reasons, to prevent any studies and my PC work (writing my book about breathing and health, updating my website www.normalbreathing.com[1], writing articles about the Buteyko oxygenation method, etc.). They did it using allergens so that I could study for one day in some university study room or a library, but the next day this place

---

1.   http://www.normalbreathing.com/

would be sprayed with allergic substances that create variety of health symptoms.

2007-2008 events included old intelligent toys: sleep deprivation, allergic gases, creation of migraines, social isolation, theft and manipulation of emails, asking hundreds of people about actions of sabotage, delays, meanness, cheating, deception, etc.

Differences from medieval rope pulling torture. Developments in technology and toxicology helped the agents to refine the methods of GI poisoning and control. During middle ages, the victim either died, in the course of days or weeks, or had severe problems for the rest of the (short) life. Now many unpleasant factors and elements of this torture method are excluded.

First, the agents use secret cameras and remain hidden from the person, while in the past the torturers were in close proximity to the person. Second, instead of using the rope (physical evidence), the secret agents employ chemicals, bacteria, viruses, worms and other parasites that are difficult to detect and present as evidence. Third, while middle age torturers were observing the blood on the rope and immediate first pain, the chemicals makes the work of the secret agents "clean" (no visible blood). Forth, subsequent secret observation of the person by the agents makes chances or recovery diminished to zero. The intelligence of the agents can be directed to control the degree of the digestive distress. Fifth, while the middle age activities are called the "torture methods", now they are "special methods".

Why did creation of GI problems become popular among some NSAs?

1. The person has burping, produce gas and, hence, feels socially uncomfortable and isolated from relatives, friends and any human community. Participation in any social gathering can result in public embarrassment.

2. The person cannot even walk normally. Walking must be very slow. That also makes him feel socially isolated and physically incapacitated. Should he walk normally or run, digestive distress creates the symptoms of flare up (diarrhea, burping, gas, pain, etc.), including psychological and physiological distress.

3. Detection and prove of poisoning is nearly impossible since the agents use poisons with extreme potency. Minuscule amounts of these poisons are required in order to successfully do the job. Poisoning with bacteria, viruses and worms, on the other hand, might be "explained" by natural causes.

4. Many months or even years are required in many countries in order to conduct endoscopies and other intrusive investigation that can identify various digestive problems or, for example, kidney disease.

5. Generally, blood tests, X-rays, EKGs, EEGs, and various other scans and tests are conducted by special laboratories. The agents have unlimited access to any state or private facility and can make any changes in lab reports, since the agents control all computers.

Hence, it is virtually impossible to prove the use of toxic or poisonous chemicals by the agents. Even if such chemicals are officially found, these chemicals never have the mark or signature of their users. All previous evidence and artifacts were stolen or disappeared. Among them are medical history files, X rays, EEGs, faxes, letters, and various lab reports.

Practical results. There are the following results of united efforts of various NSA agents in health area.

Chapter 2. Oath of secrecy and its impact on behavior of secret agents

* 2023 comment. This paper probably had another title "Why and how national securities choose and make their agents scoundrels".

Keywords: national security agency, security intelligence, social role, negative and positive secrecy, social implications, conditioning, social behavior, hiding villain effect, social conformity, protection and abuses, abuse of power, corruption, cover-up, fear.

Abstract

National security agencies perform many exceptionally important and useful social functions, including protection of airports, chemical, bacteriological, viral and other weapons, including nuclear bombs and explosives, transportation, factories, etc. These are the activities which the agents themselves are proud about and will not mind their recording for future. This paper addresses psycho roots of those activities of some agents, which they try to hide even from their colleagues and which traces are never found even in their own classified literature. Hiring and work in many national security agencies is influenced by social implications attached to the notion of secrecy or secrecy forever, and practically can be expressed as a "hiding villain" effect, when unconscious goal of the agent is to get involved in such activities and situations so that to generate the need to hide from other people later and live in constant fear.

Q: During the process of recruitment of a new agent, he signs an Oath of Secrecy, his activities and many other parameters of his life would be "secret forever". What are the possible reactions of the new agent?

A: Since the NSAs (national security agencies) are searching for smart, educated, and gifted people, who normally have some aspirations or even life ambitions, this idea of secrecy forever can produce strong emotions since the life plans are now to be changed. Likely, many agents would experience emotional torments or angst when making a choice to join the NSA.

Existence of emotional angst indicates that there is something else, on a deeper level, going on. In normal situations, when there is nothing to be fearful about or when people experience or find something positive or emotionally uplifting (mutual love, great job, winning a contest, making a discovery, creating amazing pieces of arts, etc.) there are no psycho torments, just a pure uninhibited joy. Hence, presence, degree and duration of the angst in the agent can tell us something about unconscious decision of the agent to have such goals and behavior so that they will result in fear.

If the angst are present, it is likely that the agent makes a shift from the previous life plans/ideas/projects (with the socially useful goal to excel in sciences, business, arts, hobbies, etc.), to a new mode of behaviour based on historico-social perception of secrecy. There are many components in this spiritual change: for example, past aspirations were based on win-win outcomes (so that both he and others would benefit from his accomplishments in science, art, business, sports, social work, etc.); the new aspirations of the agent would relate to modern popular implications attached to understanding of secrecy.

Q: What would be the new ruling principles for these agents?

A: This depends on degree of angst, modern popular perception of secrecy, wisdom of the agent to feel or see it, confidence of the people who hire him, and many other factors. Modern social life, movies (e.g., Star Wars, westerners, and suspense movies), ancient Greek stories, and most other sources provide situations where secrecy is usually a feature of villains, scoundrels, liars, etc. with corresponding behaviour. Thus, during an ordinary life, a person hears thousands of stories about this type of secrecy and little about positive secrecy in a spiritual sense. (Secrecy related to technological processes, which is normal in science, corporations, patenting, finances, military affairs, etc., is not discussed here.)

Q: Are there many spiritually positive examples of secrecy?

A: They are exceptionally rare. There were some stories, popular during Soviet times, about some Soviet pioneers, about 12-14 years old school boys, who would secretly visit others with special intentions. They would choose, for example, an elderly woman, who had no one to help her and secretly weed her garden or chop her wood, and disappear so that she would not be able to see them near her house. Hence, there are people and behaviours when a person does something good to another and the doer does not seek any rewards and even withdraws so that the receiver of goodness does not know whom to thank. It is also a stunning example of personal modesty and good will.

Sometimes, rich people can provide anonymous donations, but (often?) these people could be driven by guilt or shame about the methods of getting those riches. Volunteers are usually on the surface (they get public attention) so their situations are different. Hiding Jews during WW2 genocide had some similarities in relation to secrecy for the outside world, but the

Jews of course knew their saviours. Hence, we see that generally positive secrecy is exceptionally rare personal quality or trait. Some situations among family members do have some similarities, for example, when parents prepare a Christmas gift for a child "blaming" Santa Claus later.

Q: What are modern or popular implications of secrecy?

A: Traditional secrecy associates with hiding from other people due to some unpleasant or negative motives, e.g., crimes, theft, revolutionary plots to take power, avoidance of responsibility (with fear and guilt), etc. Possibly, there are many other groups of people (some sects, Jesuits?) who were also developing in similar conditions, as secret agents, after accepting a special Oath that includes secrecy elements. It could be interesting then to study what are the effects of this factor ("secrecy forever game") on their behaviour. Hence, the modern social norms imply that secrecy belongs to villains (or scoundrels).

Q: When the new agents are hired and signed the Oath of Secrecy, what happens next?

A: The supervisors are likely to emphasize other aspects of the job: special nature, vicious enemies, availability of huge info about the society, technological discoveries, etc. These factors and their emphasis on secrecy, without dealing with the implied public perception of secrecy, trigger the unconscious program of behavior that is based on social dogmas and attitudes. Hence, the new agent, by default, can take these popular standards of own future actions for granted. Presence of emotional angst is the direct and clear confirmation that the new pre-programmed behavior is in action. Let me call this situation the HV (hiding villain) effect. Obviously, it is not the huge amount of technical stuff, or super knowledge but spiritual implications which will shape the future of the agents and their ability to deal with real life challenges.

Any signs of suspicion, mistrust, or discomfort from the to-be-hired candidate would be understood as hostility or unsuitability for the job, although the roots of this psychological discomfort are in the HV effect. Hence, only "suitable" candidates, who were socially programmed by the HV effect, are accepted as new secret agents. Moreover, if there are pathological scoundrels or villains, they can experience enthusiasm and zeal when the rules of the game ("secrecy forever") are explained. The interviewer then may get an impression that this candidate is most suitable. Hence, hiring new agents can become a game: fishing for scoundrels and villains.

Hence, in future, the minds of agents unconsciously choose such behaviour so that it would indeed be necessary and sensible for them to hide from people around them. This idea "you are to remain secret forever" is another initial situational factor that drives the agents in certain direction, disregarding their initial differences and personal traits.

Q: Is it possible to analyze the HV effect mentally or in practical settings?

A: One may consider various relevant scenarios. What would be the likely spiritual developments of the agent, if he is said during the process of hiring and/or informed later?

Scenario 1. "Everything what you do, who you are, your real name, relatives, etc. will be forever unknown to others, even to future agents. You will have full and absolute protection."

Scenario 2. "Everything what you do will be video recorded for future purposes (for other agents to learn from and our internal purposes). However, you will be physically totally protected: your name, whereabouts, relatives, etc. will be forever unknown to others, even to future agents. You may even get later an identity of the some deceased person. Thus, everything that is done by the person on this particular position will be either the pride, or shame, or so-so of the agency and our nation"?

Scenario 1 is obviously based on theatrical melodramatism since it is implied that the current inventors of the secrecy-forever idea have such super-brains that they are able to predict all future historical developments and know what will be secret in future.

These are probably 2 extremes, while the life can offer many other variations since, likely, NSAs of different countries use different approaches and it could be interesting to investigate the relationship between these typical initial words and future behaviour of the agents. This paper suggests that there is an effect of sensitive dependence in initial conditions.

Q: Which activities will be normal for the "hiding villain"?

A: The HV effect robes the agents from these goals providing them with goals that are typical for scoundrels and villains. Hence, they unconsciously accept similar standards, pastime, and pleasures. It can be expected then that instead of having meaningful life and be in control, the agents, in the psychological or spiritual area, become "free artists" where goal is to have entertainment (if nobody watches and salary is flowing, why not to relax?). The objects and subjects of the entertainment will be other people, various human groups, machinery, electrical and mechanical devices, helicopters, planes, drugs, poisons, viruses, toxins, sleep deprivation, theft and manipulation of electronic communication, emotions and feelings of others, their health, jobs, housing, families, social isolation, or everything which the agents can reach within their territorial area, plus some extracurricular activities, or activities outside the own territory.

It would be a daily mental challenge for the agents to generate such fantasies and act accordingly so that it would be necessary to hide from other people and live in fear in future. If there is no fear, then there is no need to hide. Hence, formation of fear, at least on unconscious level, is a necessary factor of the HV effect and corresponding actions.

Chapter 3. KGB in the past: dealing with the general public

Now it is known more about different countries where many people were persecuted and killed for their nationality, beliefs and political activities against former ruling governments (USSR and Germany, China and Laos, countries in Africa and Latin America). For example, during 1930's in the USSR Stalin's regime killed millions of Soviet people. Meanwhile, well over 95% of Soviet adult population at any moment of time from 1930's till late 1980's had no idea about such a scale of massacres. How was it possible to involve and organize some people in secret killings and persecution of others, or just to make most people silent about violations of basic human rights?

Let me consider typical situations which took place during Stalin's time in the USSR. Everything usually started with a letter-complaint (often anonymous) to a communist leader or security agent about activity or a single act of some person against the existing social order. The decision about guilt, persecutions or even death sentence were secretly accepted by three people (security agents and party leaders). Depending on the official rank of the accused or suspected person, the KGB predecessors employed security agents of different ranks.

The involvement of ordinary people by agents often began with their meeting and had a following typical scenario. The agent(s) delivered a speech in very confident manner about tense international situation, sabotage actions organized by enemies in the country, necessity of constant alertness, extra importance of security agents, urgency of their business, and necessity of customer's participation. This emotional approach with concentration on irrelevant information was in contrast with the methods used by lawyers, doctors, policemen, emergency and military workers, where objective rational business-like communication was a key to the solution of important and urgent problems.

After the speech, the security agent(s) could ask the customer to give evidence against some person, spread rumours, terminate employment of the person, sign the letter of condemnation and/or the pledge of faithfulness to the regime while keeping the whole business as a state secret. The secrecy was justified by superior importance of the problem and presence of atrocious enemies around.

Some customers enthusiastically participated in those persecutions and were reliable confederates. Often these people were quickly promoted either as administrators or formal and informal agents, since they could easily grasp the rules of the game and the idea to secretly act behind human backs were attractive to them. Customers with more straight thinking could either believe to the agent(s) (who was an authority from the government) and with some doubts and anxiety were able to do whatever was required. The last (rare) case was when the customer refused to do anything against the persecuted person because either of own beliefs and/or knowledge of the persecuted. Then this customer could be announced as a "traitor/enemy of the Motherland" and the same activity of agents took place against him/her. In few cases, that led to formation of groups of resistance and famous "Lawsuit against doctors", "Lawsuit against scientists", "Lawsuit against politicians".

The pledge of faithfulness or secrecy agreement provided an excellent cover-up. Indeed, any open information exchange could damage the immaculate reputation of the agency. Its image were also protected by inner investigations when there were too many complaints about obvious wrong-doing (e.g., rape, bribery, torture of informers). Rumours were targeted on social isolation of the persecuted. Letters of condemnations were published in central Soviet newspapers and were common only for those persecuted who achieved highest reputation in science, arts, military or political affairs. These letters were supposed to demonstrate unshaken unity of Soviet people:

"We, leading writers (poets, scientists, musicians) of the Soviet Union condemn recent works of ...(the persecuted's name) for his(her) anti-Communist tendencies. With pain in our hearts we also found that he(she) became a capitalist agent who cooperated with our enemies ...(Numerous signatures).((Now one can guess how these signatures were obtained))". Such letters were often long but just repeated the same emotional ideas and did not have any factual criticism. The country was flooded with alert informers many of whom had a main life goal to eavesdrop and persecute "traitors". As a result, the government secret machine could quickly repress any "astray-going" person. The persecuted were usually taken in the middle of the night (less witnesses and the half-awaked victim) in a black limousine with about 5-7 gunmen. According to different estimates Stalin's regime got rid of from 10 to 20 millions of "spies" and "enemies", while dark 1937 yielded about 1 million.KGB in the past: dealing with the general public

Now it is known more about different countries where many people were persecuted and killed for their nationality, beliefs and political activities against former ruling governments (USSR and Germany, China and Laos, countries in Africa and Latin America). For example, during 1930's in the USSR Stalin's regime killed millions of Soviet people. Meanwhile, well over 95% of Soviet adult population at any moment of time from 1930's till late 1980's had no idea about such a scale of massacres. How was it possible to involve and organize some people in secret killings and persecution of others, or just to make most people silent about violations of basic human rights?

Let me consider typical situations which took place during Stalin's time in the USSR. Everything usually started with a letter-complaint (often anonymous) to a communist leader or security agent about activity or a single act of some person against the existing social order. The decision about guilt, persecutions or even death sentence were secretly accepted by three people (security agents and party leaders). Depending on the official rank of the accused or suspected person, the KGB predecessors employed security agents of different ranks.

The involvement of ordinary people by agents often began with their meeting and had a following typical scenario. The agent(s) delivered a speech in very confident manner about tense international situation, sabotage actions organized by enemies in the country, necessity of constant alertness, extra importance of security agents, urgency of their business, and necessity of customer's participation. This emotional approach with concentration on irrelevant information was in contrast with the methods used by lawyers, doctors, policemen, emergency and military workers, where objective rational business-like communication was a key to the solution of important and urgent problems.

After the speech, the security agent(s) could ask the customer to give evidence against some person, spread rumours, terminate employment of the person, sign the letter of condemnation and/or the pledge of faithfulness to the regime while keeping the whole business as a state secret. The secrecy was justified by superior importance of the problem and presence of atrocious enemies around.

After the death of Stalin (1953), new party leaders rehabilitated many names, the agency (now under the name KGB) also changed its tactic. Indeed, during 30's the person could be killed for accidental stepping on Stalin' s photo in a newspaper during a street walk, or for a single disapproving remark or anecdote about communist leaders. During late 1950's and afterwards the repressive apparatus turned mainly against dissidents and Jews. Instead of killing, security agents employed more sophisticated methods.

Many dissidents were detained in mental hospitals with an explanation, "If he criticizes socialism, he must be mentally sick". Dissidents were often on drugs and under constant pressure to sign papers with refusal from their ideas. In more than 100 "hard" dissident cases, doctors performed lobotomy. Interestingly to note, that Soviet neurologists had good understanding that the removal of the frontal lobes of the brain was the same as elimination of the flee will (with such elements as planning ahead, higher order logical thinking, control of behavior and instincts) and was equal to reducing a person to a vegetable while preserving the human body (later such person could be shown to others, "Look. he is fine"). Thus, this operation was performed in the USSR only on dissidents, whereas in the USA and other western countries some doctors made money doing exactly the same operation while claiming that they were treating schizophrenia or excessive aggression.

More subtle methods used in dealing with customers evolved too. The presentation of KGB policy became an art, where the whole speech was designed by the most experienced and skillful orators and learned by other agents by rote with numerous rehearsals to ensure confident body language, friendly voice and sympathetic facial expressions. Real meetings with customers were often secretly recorded in order to analyze the agent's performance and customer's reaction. The rate of success in dealing with customers and in breaking dissidents were the most important parameters for job promotions within the agency. Indeed, the same qualities of persuasion were required for KGB leaders to deal with government officials (to ask for money, to divert scandals, to involve these officials into security business, etc.). As one can expect, that led to advancement of people with either intrinsically silly or trustworthy facial expressions and body language.

The first step of customers, signing of the paper indicating either the desire to secretly cooperate with the agency or secrecy of all actions became the major tool of behavior control and attachment to the KGB. This act again took place immediately at the end of the emotional, often long, speech when most customers were confused and anxious. Note that, then usual confidentiality agreements are signed (e.g., by scientists or businessmen), people spend days if not weeks thinking about each letter and comma, which information to protect, from whom, with whom, how long, etc.. This secret document was similar to a marriage forever without the right to divorce or to complain to others. In addition, the customer was not going to get any real secrets.

The confusion of customers was created by a dissonance between decent superficial behavior of the agent and his irrational speech. Indeed, if one would analyze it in written form (by the way, its recording was never permitted by agents), post-analysis would easily reveal its hysterical or paranoiac nature (here is some parallel with Hitler's speeches: very convincing in the past, but not now).

Later the agent could play a fool, absent-minded intelligent who needed help, strict teacher, or moody clown. The rule was never to mention the signing situation (except agreement's violations, of course) but to displace customer's anxiety and confusion into new problems as well as create as much confusion as possible. For example, the agents often gave such information about the persecuted so that to direct the imagination of customers in inventing atrocious plots which could exist in the heads of the persecuted (e.g., to kill political leaders, to organize bloody contra-revolutions, to poison people, or to take power). This last idea about taking power was frequently ascribed to Jews who were prevented from job promotions, and many their achievements in different areas (science, art, medicine) were suppressed.

Some customers felt that their previous behavior (signing of the paper) was not smart and responsible step. Thus, they tried to compensate it by playing "responsibility" (in respect to agents' needs) now. This desire were employed to eavesdrop others, be an informer, or perform tricks against the persecuted. Simplest strange, hostile or even positive actions towards the persecuted (not mentioning lying, cheating, stealing, spreading rumours, bureaucratic tricks, employment termination) were considered by agents as a success due to customer' s additional bonding to the agency and alienation with the persecuted since these tricks required mental justifications of customers (these small initial, even seemingly neutral steps to involve people in any activity are called, in social psychology, "channel factors"). In many cases customers were asked to perform dirty tricks (depending on their initial "abilities") against the persecuted people. It is not difficult to guess how agents used different wording in order to justify these actions. Here are few possible scenarios.

1. "Who is a person? How to find his real nature? During everyday life all people are almost the same, they eat, sleep, work... We have to invent something unusual and stressful to check him. What you can suggest ..."

2. "What are the most important qualities in humans? Why do people commit crimes? Because they do not have tolerance towards others. We are dealing with this person for a long time. The tolerance is the quality which he definitely needs. He must be tolerant towards mistakes of others. Which "mistake" you can do?"

3. "We use some special methods in our work (your job is to invent from them some theories about the guilt and atrocious intentions of the enemy). Could you help us to ...?"

In all these cases, the goal of the agent, in relation to responsibility, was to form a union with the customer under the slogan "whatever you do under our supervision, we are responsible, but you have to be silent about us".

As a result of such meetings and organized media propaganda, a dissident was considered in the post-Stalin USSR as a nuisance (he could get sympathies mainly from the West), and most his acquaintances were unable of any sincere communication with him (their job was to suspect, persecute or eavesdrop). Often the agent recruited many informers who were spying after each other without suspicion that they worked for the same agent. Such "checking" in absence of "real" enemies could keep informers in shape, as agents believed. Special agent-invented actions of such informers provided such agents with some entertainment.

If a customer refused to do whatever was required after signing, he/she would get troubles from agents. The next day he could find a dead animal or bird in front of his house. His work supervisor would inform him (with compassion!) about a possibility of bad events for the customer. Back at home he could find some devices broken or malfunctioning. If he would mention the possible involvement of the agency to anybody else, they would ask why it was done. If he would explain about his refusal, it would be a violation of the secrecy. If he complained to any officials that somebody was harassing him, he could be sent to the mental hospital.

Some customers invented their escape routes from commitment, such as severe illness or moving to another part of the country. Paradoxically, most customers blamed anything except the KGB and themselves for these problems even years later, e.g. in 1990's.

Industrial espionage in other countries was another normal KGB practice. The agency tried to involve in it almost every Soviet scientist who was going abroad. In 1991-1992, I had my own experience dealing with four KGB officers when I had a chance to work in the Technical Research Centre of Finland (note that Finland was the most friendly western country for the USSR). One of the officers resided in the Moscow State University where I worked before my departure, three others represented a "scientific group" in Soviet Embassy in Helsinki. Their speeches were very long (one of the additional reasons was "every country is doing that"). Their desire to make me steal something for them and sign some papers was very strong, as well as my confusion and anxiety afterwards. My visits to them were a necessary condition of other Soviet bureaucrats who were responsible for issuing me single visas ("carrots") to travel abroad and back to Moscow.

I stole nothing for them and during my first month of work informed my Finnish supervisor about these KGB's attempts (I still believe that it was a right thing to do). The next day, I was questioned by Finnish secret police. They knew all these KGB people and their activities too. The investigators were just sad about my problems (I had to lie to KGB officers that it was totally impossible to steal any important ideas from the laboratory). As it turned out, to my immense relief, these capitalists were not as bad as the KGB painted them. They did not ask me to sign anything, to steal, or to cheat on KGB agents.

The Constitution (which did not include freedom of beliefs, thoughts and their expressions, but had many other freedoms and rights, like to get education, health care, be employed) was claimed to be the main law and could be found almost in each building framed on walls. Meanwhile, the work of such repressive apparatus was possible due to special rights of agents. If one would translate these rights from internal documents and acts on the everyday language, they could enter any place any time and do whatever they wanted (obviously, including criminal actions and those in contradiction with the Constitution).

Paradoxically, even now, western and almost all other countries still delegate unlimited rights to national security agencies. They are not only gathering and passing information to other government authorities, but themselves decide if a person is a "threat to national security" or not and how to punish him using "special methods" (dirty tricks). They can and do use drugs, viruses, bacteria, intestinal worms, poisonous gases, etc.. As a result, one can conclude that, so far, little has been learned from our recent history.

Chapter 4. Root causes of the war (my political views on nature and activities of national security agencies)

In 1994 one of my family members was brain-washed by KGB-related people. There were hundreds of Soviet and Russian people on whom secret experiments with mind control were done. Some other Russian people I personally knew died (many were about 25-30 years old). Since it was silly to expect help from Russian state officials (they were all KGB-controlled), I conducted my own investigations and found that many foreigners were also brainwashed and many others died in mysterious situations in countries and places where these KGB-related people travelled years ago.

During the same year, 1994, I informed consulates and embassies of a few involved countries so that to prevent future cases of brainwashing and provide safety for people world-wide. Also, in 1994 I immigrated to Canada. However, the organizers of mind control activities (let me call them "the Mafia", a part of the KGB) found out about my revelations and they became very upset and frustrated about that.

As one may imagine, my knowledge about the "intelligent kitchen" (or what they cook), "artistic paintings" (with hundreds dead worldwide due to plane crashes, industrial "accidents", traffic "disasters", etc.), and psychological or "special" activities of agents, made national security agencies of many countries very upset, since I was and am exposing the dirty tricks which they routinely organize on a mass scale using a wide variety of methods and techniques. This is only a part of the hatred that I experienced during these years from secret agents. There is more to it. And this part relates to the Mafia which included parts of Russian and Canadian secret agents.

The Mafia has chosen the following tactic for their revenge. When they find that a certain person is helping me in any way, the Mafia can kill relatives of this person as a "punishment" for interactions with me. I discovered this tactic about 1 year ago since many of my friends lost their close relatives in some strange circumstances (due to activities of the Mafia). In some young families I personally knew, the Mafia people killed very young children testifying about the degree of courage and bravery of the Mafia.

I found myself in the situation which was typical for persecuted Jews during WW2 (Nazi were also killing those who helped Jews to hide or escape).

My life, therefore, involves a lot of travelling and keeping low profile about my whereabouts and new contacts (so that even my closest relatives have no idea where I am now). However, there is always a risk of exposure since the Mafia managed to have good internet control and the Mafia keeps in fear all NSAs (national security agencies), including the CIA, FBI, MI-5, and many others who try to defend own countries and fight with this sophisticated type of terrorism that involves brain-washing.

During about 10 years of travelling in many countries, simply due to harassment and persecutions, of the Western agents, I found that the Mafia also organized crimes in those countries and places where I stayed so that to condition local secret agents, like dogs, against me. Hence, local secret agents were always in a difficult situation when I was around. (There is a paper below that describes the psychology of the spiritual war between Nazi and Jews during WW2.)

Therefore, based on attached papers, one may realize that the root causes of the war waged by many national security organizations of western countries against me is in the totally different, often opposite understanding of public safety and national security. Most agents worldwide view the domestic or normal national security organization as an agency that collect and uses dirty tricks, poisons, toxins, sleep deprivation, radiation, allergens and conditioning to allergies, worms, bacteria, viruses, heavy metals and all other chemicals that are forbidden to use even during the war; avoiding any responsibility; sulkiness in relation to public media; secrecy in relation to own people; and absence of any control and recorded evidence or history of activities of the secret agents. My vision is opposite: absence of dirty tricks; criminal responsibility for drugging and use of toxins and poisons; secrecy of other people but transparency in relation to secret agents; complete video-recorded information about all paid or job-related activities of the secret agents (for internal purposes and future references).

Chapter 5. Development of new clandestine methods and techniques by national security organizations to destroy human health, well-being, and life

There are some unique torture/health destruction techniques that are secretly used by national security agents in the USA, Canada, the UK, Ireland, the Netherlands, Belgium, Italy, and possibly some other western countries. I practically experienced these methods and conducted my own research about physiological effects of these techniques.

1) Secret sleep deprivation (using clicking noises that do not wake up the person, but eliminate deep stages of sleep and can reduce the person to a vegetable state or easily kill him. Mild application of this method causes daytime sleepiness, inability to concentrate, sleep apnoea, forgetfulness, irritation, appearance of nervous, digestive, and many other problems. Many days of such secret sleep deprivation resulted in loss of hunger, extreme irritability emotional instability, and death in experimental animals. [Sleep apnoea, a potentially fatal condition, rate had dramatic increase in certain countries during the last decade. I do know about secret application of night noises by Californian FBI agents. They subjects developed severe sleep apnoea. The tiny devices produce clicking noises due to an electromagnetic signal send from outside, similar to a cell phone.]

2) Secret allergic conditioning to paper ink (so that just 2-3 breaths of air when reading a book or a fresh newspaper

will cause severe migraine headache for many hours). Such conditioning can be done by poisoning the food with ink or during nights when the organism is conditioned by two gases: one for headache and another as ink gas. As a result of this method, if the person opens a newspaper or a book, he will get headache for the remaining part of the day. The person will not be able to go to libraries or copy shops. Fear will rule his life. Traveling in buses or trains will be a huge health hazard. [During such trips, "smart" intelligent agents can provide other passengers with free newspapers; I experienced this myself.]

3) Secret allergic conditioning to weak electromagnetic field (the person is radiated using a moderate dose of radiation to condition the immune system against any source of electromagnetic waves.). Weeks later even an ordinary lamp in a room will cause an allergic response in the "controlled" subject. Any trip near electrical cables (but they are almost everywhere!) will result in allergic response depending on the individual health state. It can be an asthma attack, heart attack, severe migraine, epilepsy attack, stroke, digestive distress, arthritis pain, itching due to eczema, etc.

3) Secret allergic conditioning to detergents, pesticides, herbicides, bleaches, paints, and household, garden and other poisons, toxins and chemicals

Since modern leaders of western national security organizations to not provide their agents with poisons, while local agents have absolute freedom and no any control in using any method or poison, many agents started to use toxic chemicals that are very potent and can be bought in ordinary hardware and gardening store sand shops. The person is fed any of the above-mentioned substances for days or weeks so that his immune system gets conditioned and any exposure to the same chemical later will produce the allergic reaction or an acute attack. For example, if a person later starts sleeping on a pillow that was washed by the same detergent that he ate for weeks, the smell or skin contact with tiny amounts of the detergent will cause an allergic reaction or an acute episode. Similarly, breathing air in parks (sprayed with pesticides or herbicides) will also cause corresponding health problems.

Moreover, it will be easy later for the agents to generate pain and distress in this person by spraying corresponding toxins and affecting only him even though the person can be in a large crowd of people since only he will be affected. In all these cases, the person is even unlikely to guess or suspect that all these health problems were created by secret agents.

Please, inform other organizations and people about these intelligent "developments" and feel free to copy this paper.

Chapter 6. My 2008 letters and emails to various human right officials

6.1 Addresses and emails of Human rights watch officials

E-mail info@amnesty.de
350 Fifth Avenue, 34th floor
New York, NY 10118-3299, USA
Tel: 1-(212) 290-4700, Fax: 1-(212) 736-1300
hrwnyc@hrw.org
1630 Connecticut Avenue, N.W., Suite 500
Washington, DC 20009, USA
Tel:1-(202) 612-4321, Fax:1-(202) 612-4333
hrwdc@hrw.org
11500 W. Olympic Blvd., Suite 441
Los Angeles, CA 90064, USA
Tel:1-(310) 477-5540, Fax: (310) 477-4622
hrwla@hrw.org
Human Rights Watch
100 Bush Street, Suite 1812
San Franzisko, CA 94104, USA
Tel: 415.362.3250, Fax: 415.362.3255
hrw-sf@hrw.org
Human Rights Watch
Poststraße 4-5
10178 Berlin, Germany
Tel. +49-(0)30-259306-10

Fax. +49-(0)30-259306-29
berlin@hrw.org
Avenue des Gaulois, 7
1040 Brüssel, Belgien
Tel: 32 (2) 732-2009
Fax: 32 (2) 732-0471
hrwatcheu@skynet.be
9 rue Cornavin
1201 Genf, Schweiz
Tel: +41 22 738 04 81
Fax: +41 22 738 17 91
hrwgva@hrw.org
2nd Floor, 2-12 Pentonville Road
London N1 9HF, Großbritannien
Tel: 44 20 7713 1995, Fax: 44 20 7713 1800
hrwuk@hrw.org
2300 Yonge Street
Suite 803, Box 2376
Toronto, Ontario M4P-1E4
Kanada
toronto@hrw.org
Human rights watch
berlin@hrw.org

6.2 My letters "Health-destruction and secret torture methods used by western secret agents"

RE: Health-destruction and secret torture methods used by western secret agents

Dear Sir/Madam,

I am a Canadian citizen for over 10 years. Please find enclosed my information about violations of human rights, torture, and health destruction methods practiced by national security agents in Canada, the USA, Ireland, the UK, Belgium, Holland, and Italy during my travel and stay in these countries. Feel free to publish any of the enclosed documents in press for public awareness or to share them with proper international organizations.

I am currently in Germany and interested in my physical and medical examination in order to find out practical evidence of the health-destructive activities of secret agents from these countries. I applied for political asylum in Ireland (1998, 2001), Norway (1998, 2000, 2005), the UK (2000, 2001), Finland (2004), Holland (2003), etc., but all officials of these countries claimed that Canada is a safe country and no proper medical examination were done there (no tests at all).

Is there a possibility to have medical examination in relation to following health problems I have now or had in the past (I believe that all these problems resulted from special operations of secret agents):

1) severe allergy to electromagnetic fields (an ordinary lamp in a room will cause an allergic reaction, walking on the streets and being near electrical cables causes allergic reaction)

2) headache due to paper ink (reading a newspaper or a book for 1 minute is enough for the migraine to appear so that for the rest of the day any activity, especially mental ones, is difficult)

3) abnormal sleeping pattern, abnormal sensitivity to noises at night and negative effects of clicking noises (as a result of months of sleep deprivation)

4) multiple kidney failure

5) multiple liver failure

6) severe gastritis and irritable bowel syndrome

7) neurological effects of poisoning with mercury and aluminum (decreased short term memory, etc.)?

If you cannot help with tests, do you know any other organization or group in Germany that can organize testing in order to expose the methods used by secret agents in those Western countries?

My email address: artour_rakhimov@hotmail.com

Sincerely,

Artour Rakhimov (PhD, citizen of Canada, born on 21 July 1964).

Enclosures

Personal experience about war on terrorism, as it is practiced by national security agencies (8 pages)

Why and how national securities choose and make their agents scoundrels (2 pages)

KGB in the past: dealing with the general public (4 pages)

Root causes of the war (my political views on nature and activities of national security agencies (1 page)

Development of new methods and techniques to destroy human health, well-being, and life (1 page)

6.3 My letters about violations of human rights

Violations of human rights

The United Nations Office at Geneva

Office of the Director-General

Palais des Nations

Avenue de la Paix 8- 14

1211 Geneva 10

Switzerland

Tel: +41 (0)22 917 21 29 / 917 11 40

Fax: +41 (0)22 917 00 01

Email: llo@unog.ch[1], urgent-action@ohchr.org[2]

RE: Violations of human rights by western national securities

Dear Sir/Madam,

Please find enclosed my information about violations of human rights by national security agencies. Feel free to publish any of the enclosed documents in press for public awareness.

My home address is: 260 Fisherville Ave., North York, Ontario M2R 3C5 Canada

However, I do not know when I am going to be there since it is simply unsafe to arrive or remain for me in Canada.

---

1.   http://uk.f250.mail.yahoo.com/ym/

Compose?To=llo@unog.ch&YY=79468&y5beta=yes&y5beta=yes&order=down&so

rt=date&pos=0&view=a&head=b

2.   http://uk.f250.mail.yahoo.com/ym/

Compose?To=urgent-action@ohchr.org&YY=79468&y5beta=yes&y5beta=yes&orde

r=down&sort=date&pos=0&view=a&head=b

You may try to use my email address: artour_rakhimov@hotmail.com. However, I had numerous instances when my emails were stolen, intercepted, changed, etc.

There is now a strong campaign to intimidate me and prevent these papers from publications. These activities are generated by FBI, MI-5, Garda, and Dutch national security agencies. You may follow my life through observing changes on my website www.normalbreathing.com[3]. After years of studying own diseases and being poisoned I teach people how to be healthy.

Sincerely,

Artour Rakhimov (PhD, citizen of Canada, born on 21 July 1964).

Enclosures (all pages are signed, for safety):
(... as before ...)

---

3.   http://www.normalbreathing.com/

6.4 Violations of human rights form

* Identification of the alleged victim(s);

Artour Rakhimov, citizen of Canada, date of birth 21 July 1964

* Identification of the alleged perpetrators of the violation: Security Intelligence Organizations (or national security agencies): CSIS (Canada), FBI (USA), Garda (Ireland), British national security – MI6 (the UK), Algemene Inlichtingen- en Veiligheidsdienst (AIVD) (the Netherlands), Veilighad van de Staat (national security of Belgium), Italian National Security.

* Identification of the person(s) or organization(s) submitting the communication (this information will be kept confidential);

Artour Rakhimov, citizen of Canada, date of birth 21 July 1964

* Date and place of incident (details are enclosed)

1996-2008 Toronto, Vancouver, Ottawa, Calgary, Edmonton, Halifax (all Canada); Seattle, Los Angeles, Santa Monika, San Jose, Palo Alto, Houston, (all USA); Amsterdam, Utrecht, Rotterdam (all the Netherlands); Cork. Limerick, Galway, Ennis, Dublin (all Ireland); London, Margate, Newcastle, Gateshead, Glasgow (all the UK); Pisa (Italy), Gent and Brussel (Belgium).

* A detailed description of the circumstances of the incident in which the alleged violation occurred.

Enclosed. (Personal experience about war on terrorism, as it is practiced by national security agencies (8 pages))

6.5 My letters to Special Rapporteur on Torture

Special Rapporteur on Torture

c/o Office of the High Commissioner for Human Rights

United Nations Office at Geneva

CH-1211 Geneva 10, Switzerland

E-mail: urgent-action@ohchr.org[1]

RE: Torture Quest and torture methods used by western national security agencies

Dear Sir/Madam,

Please find enclosed my information about super intelligent methods of torture developed and practiced by western national security agencies. ...

Torture Quest Form

a. Full name of the victim;

Artour Rakhimov, citizen of Canada, date of birth 21 July 1964

b. Date on which the incident(s) of torture occurred (at least as to the month and year);

Continuing from January 1996 to August 2008 (Details are attached)

c. Place where the person was seized (city, province, etc.) And location at which the torture was carried out (if known);

Toronto, Vancouver, Ottawa, Calgary, Edmonton, Halifax (all Canada), Seattle, Los Angeles, Santa Monika, San Jose, Palo

---

1.   http://uk.f250.mail.yahoo.com/ym/

Compose?To=urgent-action@ohchr.org&YY=79468&y5beta=yes&y5beta=yes&orde

r=down&sort=date&pos=0&view=a&head=b

Alto, Houston, (all USA), Amsterdam, Utrecht, Rotterdam (all the Netherlands), Cork. Limerick, Galway, Ennis, Dublin (all Ireland), Pisa (Italy), Gent and Brussel (Belgium).

d. Indication of the forces carrying out the torture;

Security Intelligence Organizations (or national security agencies):

CSIS (Canada), FBI (USA), Garda (Ireland), British national security – MI6 (the UK), Algemene Inlichtingen- en Veiligheidsdienst (AIVD) (the Netherlands), (Veilighad van de Staat) Belgian national security, Italian national security.

e. Description of the form of torture used and any injury suffered as a result;

Use of viruses, bacteria, intestinal worms, household poisons (detergents, pesticides, herbicides, other highly toxic substances), toxins, poisons, radiation, creation of allergies to paper ink (causing horrible migraine and loss of ability to work), creation of allergy to electromagnetic fields (causing high heart rate, up to 90-100 beats per minute, diarrhea, headache and loss of ability to work), sleep deprivation using clicking noises at night (one of the scummiest techniques known to humanity), creation of allergies to wheat, gluten, dairy, tomatoes, peanuts; use of heavy and other toxic metals (mercury, lead, aluminium).

f. Identify of the person or organization submitting the report (name and address, which will be kept confidential).

Artour Rakhimov, citizen of Canada, date of birth 21 July 1964

Additional sheets should be attached where space does not allow for a full rendering of the information requested. Also, copies of any relevant corroborating documents, such as medical or police records should be supplied where it is believed that such information may contribute to a fuller accounting of the incident. Only copies and not originals of such documents should be sent.

I. Identity of the person(s) subjected to torture

A. Family Name Rakhimov

B. First and other names Artour

C. Sex: Male Female Male

D. Birth date or age 21 July 1964

E. Nationality Canadian (born in Russia, enthically - Tartar)

F. Occupation (high school teacher, research scientist, breathing teacher, health educator)

G. Identity card number (if applicable) Social Insurance Number (Canada) 510 672 033

F. Activities (trade union, political, religious, humanitarian/ solidarity, press, etc.)

Exposure of brainwashing activities of KGB leading to numerous deaths of foreigners to other countries

G. Residential and/or work address

260 Fisherville Ave., North York, Ontario M2R 3C5 Canada

Email: artour_rakhimov@hotmail.com (highly unreliable: routine theft and manipulation of email messages)

II. Circumstances surrounding torture

A. Date and place of arrest and subsequent torture

No arrests; the security agents do not need to arrest, they can create torture anywhere using poisons, toxic gases, sleep deprivation, harassment, use of machinery, and employing thousands of people (including friends, relatives, co-corkers, strangers, etc.) into actions of public disapproval, humiliation, and isolation so that any prison will look like a paradise.

B. Identity of force(s) carrying out the initial detention and/or torture (police, intelligence services, armed forces, paramilitary, prison officials, other)

C. Were any person, such as a lawyer, relatives or friends, permitted to see the victim during detention? If so, how long after the arrest?

I visited many lawyers in Canada: first, they said that they could help me, but during the next meeting they would claim the conflict of interests and refused to help.

D. Describe the methods of torture used

Enclosed

E. What injuries were sustained as a result of the torture?

Severe prostatitis; multiple kidney failure; liver failure; various infectious and viral diseases; brain damage due to mercury and aluminium; brain damage due to sleep deprivation; severe gastritis; allergy to paper ink (causing horrible migraine and loss of ability to work); allergy to electromagnetic fields (causing high heart rate, up to 90-100 beats per minute, diarrhea, headache and loss of ability to work); sleep deprivation using clicking noises at night (one of the scummiest techniques known to humanity and very popular in Canada and the USA); allergies to wheat, gluten, dairy, tomatoes, peanuts, heavy and other toxic metals (mercury, lead, aluminium).

F. What was believed to be the purpose of the torture?

Elements of entertainment (since there are no real terrorists left); confusion; paranoia; the hidden villain effect; obsession with watching me; paranoia of control; undeveloped feelings of acceptance, tolerance, and patience, inability to analyze any psychologically complicated situations. These are causes and goals at the same time since the level of spiritual development of most agents is quite low.

G. Was the victim examined by a doctor at any point during or after his/her ordeal? If so, when? Was the examination performed by a prison or government doctor?

Several doctors' reports and laboratory results were stolen by the CSIS (Canadian Security Intelligence Service)

H. Was appropriate treatment received for injuries sustained as a result of the torture?

Self-study and self-treatment with occasional visits to doctors.

I. Was the medical examination performed in a manner which would enable the doctor to detect evidence of injuries sustained as a result of the torture? Were any medical reports or certificates issued? If so, what did the reports reveal?

Very hard. The secret agents are professionally trained to destroy one's health without leaving any marks or easily detectable signs. Consider kidney failure, or liver failure, or gastric ulcers, or intestinal inflammation. Ordinary thugs beat, for example, with boots, victim's head and other body parts leaving marks; secret agents beat and destroy internal organs (hence, the name: intelligence). Another part of the training is to avoid any responsibility and hide from others.

J. If the victim died in custody, was an autopsy or forensic examination performed and which were the results?

Still kicking.

III. Remedial action

Were any domestic remedies pursued by the victim or his/ her family or representatives (complaints with the forces responsible, the judiciary, political organs, etc.)? If so, what was the result?

Useless. Tried Ontario Provincial Police many times, RCMP (Royal Canadian Mountain Police) many times, CHRC (Canadian Human Right Commission) two times, SIRC (Security Intelligence Review Committee) two times, Police in Los Angeles, Santa Monika, Amsterdam – three times, Cork (Garda) – three times, etc. All say that they can do nothing against national security agents.

Epilogue

In more recent years (or since 2009), I gradually discovered the other cause why secret agents pay exclusive attention to me and everything that is going on in my life.

This cause relates to numerous crimes (usually in the form of real-life mass killings, such as massacres, shootings, explosions, plane crashes, etc.) committed around the world and often in my vicinity by a third party: probably a single former KGB agent who organized an empire of robots (or zombies who are used for making new zombies and mass killings). I found over 30 such large crimes that were committed usually within 1-5 days after some events or activities took place in my life. You may find somewhere else my description and explanations of these events.

I also plan to describe health-destructive activities of secret agents that took place until April 2023 (when this book was compiled) from specific countries such as the USA, Germany, Poland, Spain, the Netherlands, Bulgaria, Croatia, Turkey, Serbia, Macedonia, Montenegro, Georgia, Azerbaijan, Malta, Egypt, and many others.

I discovered that modern state secret agents (or local agents) in the Western world have a large degree of freedom to decide what they can do with other people (or targets) and what they cannot do. Indeed, when dealing with their targets, a specific group or mini team of secret agents can work only a certain shift (e.g., 8 hours per day) on certain days of the week meaning that they will be replaced by some other agents, but these other agents may have different views on my role or place in the world. As a result, I discovered something that I call the "shift effect" and "weekend effect". This implies a very different treatment, method, and technique used by secret agents. Also, because of intensive traveling since 1998 and changing the geographical location allowed me to discover that specific secret agents serve only a certain area with a population usually from about 5,000 up to 10,000 people. Therefore, when secret agents appear and say to all types of officials that they represent "national security", this is already a lie. In my view, they may represent "national security" when they warn or teach pilots or police people, or bus drivers about dangers hidden in interactions with unknown sexy females or other people who could be zombie-makers.

As for having order within the security intelligence community, one can contact watchdog organizations which are usually created as Parliamentary Commissions Review Committees to control national secret services. Such watchdog organizations can be easily found online

After years of real-life interactions with these watchdog organizations, I believe that these state officials are supposed to control secret agents, but they have no clue about the scope of activities and modern secret agents with other organizations and what they ask them to do in the name of "national security", but without providing any details.

You may contact your watchdog organization and ask them the following questions:

- Do people from the review committee visit businesses and organizations that deal with or produce radioactive materials, infectious (viral, bacteriological, etc.) agents, and toxic or poisonous chemicals to ask officials of these businesses and organizations if secret agents acquired any of these items and how exactly it was done (with signing release papers by secret agents and other formalities or how)?

- Do people from the review committee visit businesses and organizations that deal with all types of communication (internet/network providers, phone companies, postal offices, etc.) to ask officials of these businesses and organizations if secret agents ask about their unlimited access to communication and how exactly it was done (with signing release papers by secret agents and other formalities or how)?

- Do people from the review committee visit emergency businesses and organizations that possess emergency vehicles to ask officials of these businesses and organizations if secret agents ask about the use of this machinery for some "special operations" (extracurricular activities) and how exactly it was done (with signing release papers by secret agents and other formalities or how else)?